The Complete Color Book

by Jeri A. Carroll

illustrated by Tom Foster

Colors are always something we teach to young children. It seems strange since they are already familiar with colors that we have to teach them their colors. Actually all they need is a name for something they already know.

As children learn to name the colors, they begin by using only one color name for everything or by wearing only things of one color. They seem quite self-assured with their newfound knowledge. As they learn that there are names for many other colors, confusion sets in. And then almost like magic, they seem to be able to name them all.

Somewhere in all of these activities it is hoped that this will happen.

For those children who already know the names of the colors, experiments are suggested, camouflage activities outlined, and graphing suggested.

And there are always those beautiful rainbows.

Enjoy the activities with your children. They will love them all the more.

Cover by Tom Foster

Copyright © Good Apple, 1991

ISBN No. 0-86653-585-3

Printing No. 98765432

Good Apple
1204 Buchanan St., Box 299
Carthage, IL 62321-0299

Simon & Schuster Supplementary Education Group

Table of Contents

GA1300

Introduction

Welcome to *The Complete Color Book*, a book designed for teachers of preschool, kindergarten, first, second and third grades to help children learn their colors and learn about them as well. The world itself is quite colorful, and children will become far more aware of the colors around them as they learn more about colors.

This book is designed to incorporate many different types of activities to stimulate the child's awareness of color.

CRAYONS: Children are most familiar with crayons as the media with which to make colors. The book has crayons for them to color in, surrounding a note that they take home to their parents telling them what the color of the week is (page 4). In addition, there are a few coloring sheets that require them to read the name of a color, color it in, and write the word (page 110).

For the older children there are activities that allow them to follow directions to make melted crayon pictures, sandpaper colorings, stenciled rubbings, etc. (page 98). These individual activities can be done one at a time or set up in centers with directions to the child given on a contract and an example given at the bottom.

HOME CONNECTION: Some activities incorporate help from home—if nothing more than sending something of a certain color to school in a colorful sack (page 9). Others suggest parents cook certain foods during the week, bringing their child's attention to the color (page 49).

Children also make books to read that they may take home to read to their parents or siblings (page 46).

LANGUAGE ARTS CONNECTION: Some activities tie into reading. There are stories that may be copied for each child (page 11). Children read the stories, color the pictures, cut out the pages of the book, put them in order, and make them into a take-home book to read to their parents, grandparents or siblings.

There are children's books listed for a study about rainbows (page 60).

SCIENCE CONNECTION: Some activities tie into the natural environment with children looking for specific animals in the environment (cardinals during the study of red) (page 40) or for specific colors in the flowers (page 70) or mud (see brown).

For the older children there are experiments with recording sheets. Children have to follow directions to mix colors and record their results (page 87).

Camouflage in nature is examined as children make pictures that allow animals and insects to hide in the background (page 72).

And there are those natural dyes. Dying is a fun activity that only some teachers will try (page 105).

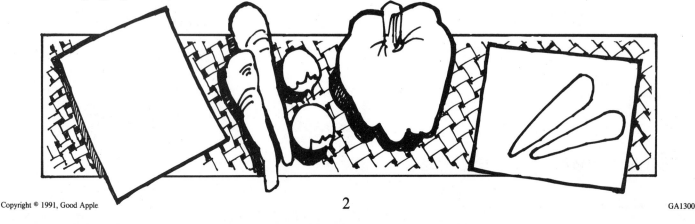

2

GA1300

MATH CONNECTION: Activities suggest graphing colors of birds (page 69), flowers (page 71), hair color (page 63), eye color (page 66).

THE FOOD CONNECTION: Although these activities are varied, they are not exactly multisensory. Color has little to do with more than one sense. There are, however, eating experiences suggested for each of the colors, both tasting parties and snacks (page 45).

Children can mix together strawberries and cream cheese to make a pink spread for a graham cracker (page 30). And then there are always the black gumdrop spiders (page 5).

Have fun with these colorful activities. The children will enjoy the marvels of color.

GA1300

black

Dear Parents:

This week we will be watching for the color black.

Your child has brought home a sack colored black. Please look around your house for something that is black to send to school. We will show the black things to the other children.

Thanks for your help.

On the first day of the time scheduled to work on the color black, have each child color a small brown sack black. Send it home with the note above. Color the crayons black before sending the note home.

When the children return the sacks, have them show what they have in them.

Make the sack into a black cat.

Stuff the bag with newspaper.

Tie a string around the top about 3″ down.

Cut the top into two parts to make two ears.

Tie them.

Place on eyes, nose and mouth.

Use black pipe cleaners for the whiskers.

Give the children a piece of white poster board with the word *black* written in such a way that they can fill in the letters. Have them color it in with glue rather than crayons. Glue on black gumdrops.

1. Trace

Trace with a crayon.

2. Glue

Fill in with glue.

3. Cover

Cover with black gumdrops.

Before the children arrive at school, cut out the letters to make the word *black*. Make each tall letter out of a 12″ x 18″ piece of paper and each small letter out of a 9″ x 12″ piece of paper. Put them up on a wall with rubber cement at a level where the children can use them.

Provide scissors and magazines, and during center time have them cut out black things from the magazines and glue them onto the letters.

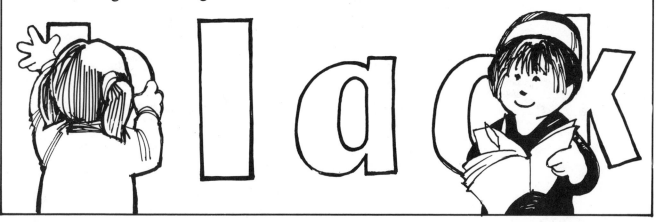

- As part of black week, have a tasting party using as many black foods as you can find. Some might say that Oreos are black. You can certainly try.

- Demonstrate how to make a spider out of a large licorice gumdrop and licorice strips. Let the children make their own. Eat them right before going home.

- During the week be sure to fly a flag denoting the color of the week. This week it could be a Batman cape or a witch's hat or cape.

- Because there are not many black food labels which the children might read, have them go on a black hunt in the school and on the playground. Record each thing they say on a piece of 4″ x 6″ white paper with black marker. When they return to the room, have them illustrate each of the things they say. Staple them together and make them into a book to place in the reading corner.

Black

1

Black as coal.

2

Black as a witch's cat.

3

Black as a tire.

4

GA1300

Black as night.

5

Black as a witch's hat.

6

Black as Batman's cape.

7

Directions:
1. Listen to the story.
2. Color the pictures.
3. Cut out the pages.
4. Put the pages in order.
5. Staple the pages.
6. Read the story.

8

GA1300

Black

This is a black

_____

This is a black

_____

This is a black

_____

This is a black

_____

8

GA1300

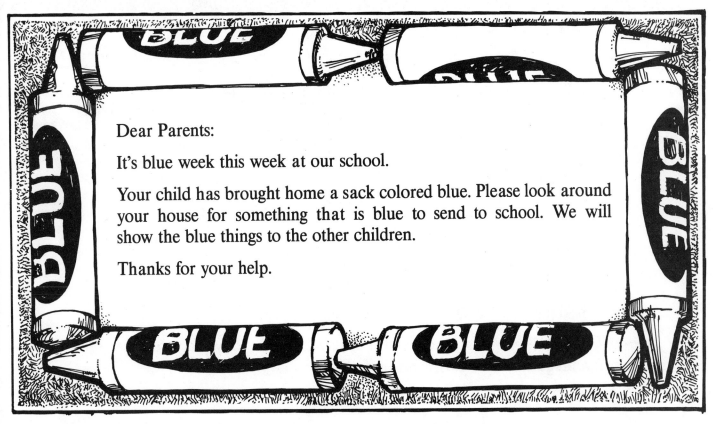

Dear Parents:

It's blue week this week at our school.

Your child has brought home a sack colored blue. Please look around your house for something that is blue to send to school. We will show the blue things to the other children.

Thanks for your help.

On the first day of the time scheduled to work on the color blue, have each child color a small brown sack blue. Send it home with the note above. Color the crayons blue before sending the note home.

When the children return the sacks, have them show what they have in them.

Make the sack into a blue bow tie.

Tie a string around the middle of the sack.

Cut off both ends.

Tie the bow tie around each boy's neck with a piece of blue yarn, or put it in each girl's hair with a clip.

Give the children a piece of white poster board with the word *blue* written in such a way that they can fill in the letters. Mix Elmer's glue with blue food coloring. Fill small bottles with the mixtures. Have the children fill in the letters with the glue.

1. Trace

Trace with a crayon.

2. Glue

Fill in with glue mixed with blue paint.

3. Feel

When dry, feel and trace.

Before the children arrive at school, cut out the letters to make the word *blue*. Make each tall letter out of a 12″ x 18″ piece of paper and each small letter out of a 9″ x 12″ piece of paper. Put them on a wall with rubber cement at a level where the children can use them.

Provide scissors and magazines, and during center time have them cut out blue things from the magazines and glue them onto the letters.

As part of blue week, have a tasting party using as many blue foods as you can find.

Demonstrate how to make a blueberry tart from an empty tart and blueberry pie filling.

If you have only flat pie crust, spread the pie filling on it like a pizza and bake 4-6 minutes.

During the week be sure to fly a flag denoting the color of the week. This week it could be a blue bandana.

Because there are not many blue food labels which the children might read, have them go outside to look at the blue sky.

Bring them back in and give them a piece of blue paper and cotton balls to make clouds. Watch as they work and ask if they can label their clouds.

Use the language pattern in It Looked Like Spilt Milk and have the children make up their own story. It looked like spilt milk, but it wasn't. It was a lamb.

GA1300

A truck can be blue.

1

2

A car can be blue.

3

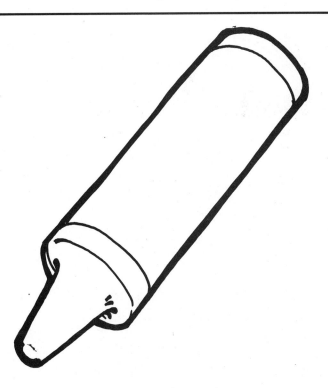

A crayon can be blue.

4

11

The sky can be blue.

5

The dress can be blue.

6

The shirt can be blue.

7

Directions:
1. Listen to the story.
2. Color the pictures.
3. Cut out the pages.
4. Put the pages in order.
5. Staple the pages.
6. Read the story.

8

GA1300

Look at this big blue

_____

drawn by _____.

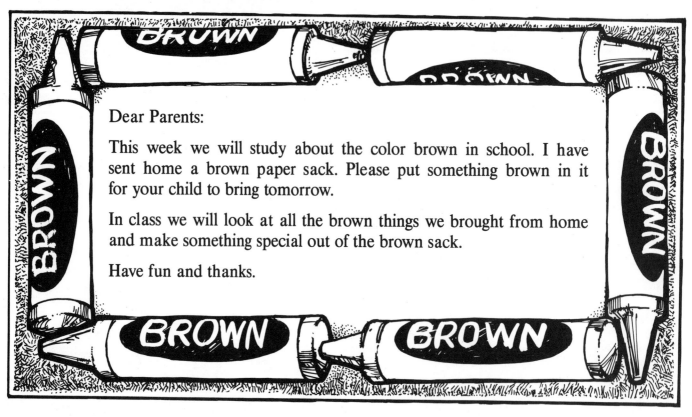

Dear Parents:

This week we will study about the color brown in school. I have sent home a brown paper sack. Please put something brown in it for your child to bring tomorrow.

In class we will look at all the brown things we brought from home and make something special out of the brown sack.

Have fun and thanks.

On the first day of the time scheduled to work on the color brown, send home a brown sack with the note above attached. Color the crayons brown before sending the note home.

When the children return the sacks, have them show what they have in them.

Make the sack into a brown puppy.

Stuff the bag with newspaper.

Tie a string around the top about 3″ down.

Cut the top into two parts.

Staple brown ears to each part.

Place on eyes, nose and mouth.

GA1300

Give the children a piece of white poster board with the word *brown* written in such a way that they will fill in the letters. Have them color it in with glue rather than crayons. Sprinkle with cocoa. When dry, feel and smell.

1. Trace

2. Glue

3. Cover

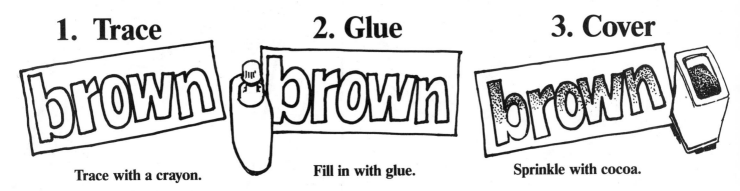

Trace with a crayon.

Fill in with glue.

Sprinkle with cocoa.

Before the children arrive at school, cut out the letters to make the word *brown*. Make each tall letter out of a 12″ x 18″ piece of paper and each small letter out of a 9″ x 12″ piece of paper. Put them on a wall with rubber cement at a level where the children can use them.

Provide scissors and magazines, and during center time have them cut out brown things from the magazines and glue them onto the letters.

As part of brown week, have a tasting party using as many brown foods as you can find. Because so much is chocolate, be sure to do it right before going home.

Demonstrate how to make chocolate toast. Let the children make their own. Eat it right before going home.

During the week be sure to fly a flag denoting the color of the week. This week it could be a brown washcloth. Have the children bring in labels that are brown which they might read.

Go on a mud walk. Make sure there are some puddles of mud. Give the children pieces of paper. When they find mud, have them draw on the paper with the mud. They could even write the words *brown* or *mud* with the mud.

15

GA1300

I colored the dirt brown.

1

2

I colored the ball brown.

3

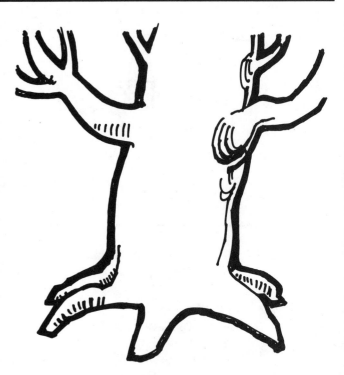

I colored the tree trunk brown.

4

16

I colored the shoe brown.

5

I colored the boot brown.

6

I colored the bunny brown.

7

Directions:
1. Listen to the story.
2. Color the pictures.
3. Cut out the pages.
4. Put the pages in order.
5. Staple the pages.
6. Read the story.

8

GA1300

Brown

_____ | _____
can be brown. | can be brown.

_____ | _____
can be brown. | can be brown.

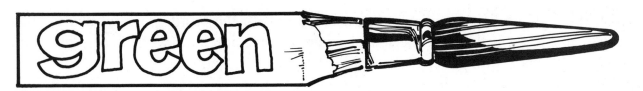

green

Dear Parents:

What green things do you have in your home? We would like to have you send at least one of those to school tomorrow in the sack your child brought home today.

Tomorrow we will look at all the green things children bring from home and hunt for green things at school. It should be fun.

Thanks.

On the first day of the time scheduled to work on the color green, send home a green paper sack with the note above attached. Color the crayons green before sending the note home.

When the children return the sacks, have them show what they have in them.

Make the sack into a monster.

Stuff the bag with newspaper.

Tie a string around the top about 3″ down.

Cut the top into two parts.

Tie them together at the top to make horns.

Make fierce eyes, nose and mouth.

GA1300

Give the children a piece of white poster board with the word *green* written in such a way that they will fill in the letters. Have them color it in with glue rather than crayons. Sprinkle with green grass clippings. When dry, feel.

1. Trace   2. Glue   3. Sprinkle   4. Feel

Trace with a crayon.   Fill in with glue.   Sprinkle with green grass.   When dry, feel.

Before the children arrive at school, cut out the letters to make the word *green*. Make each tall letter out of a 12″ x 18″ piece of paper and each small letter out of a 9″ x 12″ piece of paper. Put them up on a wall with rubber cement at a level where the children can use them.

Provide scissors and magazines, and during center time have them cut out green things from the magazines and glue them onto the letters.

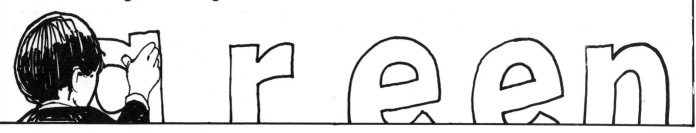

As part of green week, have a tasting party using as many green foods as you can find. Many vegetables are green so this is a really healthy party.

Demonstrate how to put a little of each vegetable into a salad bowl. Serve with green ranch dressing.

During the week be sure to fly a flag denoting the color of the week. This week it could be a green washcloth.

Have the children bring in labels that are green which the children might read.

Cut 1″ squares of green construction paper or tissue paper and make a mosaic tree.

Visit a pet shop and see all the green pets—birds, lizards, etc.

GA1300

Green

green grass

1

2

green spinach

3

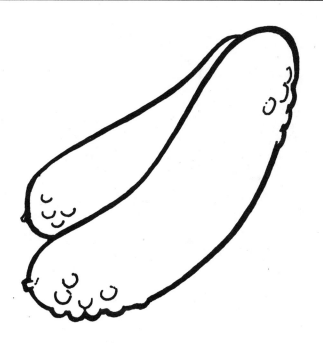

green pickles

4

GA1300

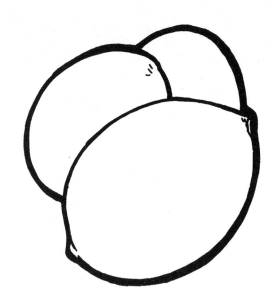

green limes

5

green beans

6

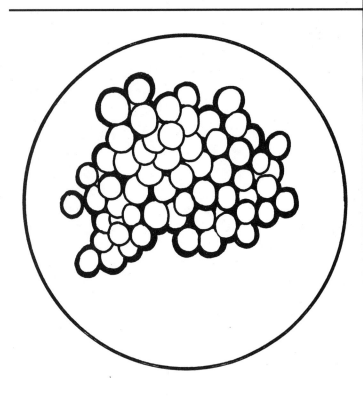

green peas

7

Directions:

1. Listen to the story.
2. Color the pictures.
3. Cut out the pages.
4. Put the pages in order.
5. Staple the pages.
6. Read the story.

8

GA1300

Green

What is green? A _____ is green.	What is green? A _____ is green.
What is green? A _____ is green.	What is green? A _____ is green.
What is green? A _____ is green.	What is green? A _____ is green.

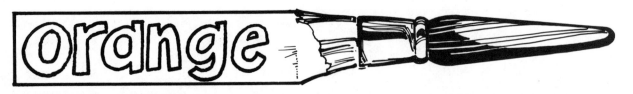

orange

Dear Parents:

Hurray for orange! It's orange week at school. The children will be doing many things this week with orange food, paper, crayons and paints.

We would like for you to send one orange thing to school in the orange sack your child brought home today. We will share these orange things tomorrow.

Thanks again for your help.

During the week before orange week, send home a white sack that each child has colored orange. Send it home with the note above. Color the crayons orange before sending the note home.

When the children return the sacks, have them show all their orange things.

When you are finished with the sack, make it into a jack-o'-lantern.

Stuff it with newspaper.

Tie a string 3″ from the top.

Glue on eyes, nose and mouth.

Hang them from the ceiling.

Give the children a piece of white poster board with the word *orange* written in such a way that they can fill in the letters. Have them fill it in with glue rather than colors. Sprinkle with orange peels. When dry, feel and smell.

1. Trace and Glue   2. Sprinkle   3. Feel

Trace with a crayon.
Fill in with glue.

Sprinkle with orange peel.

When dry, feel.

Before the children arrive at school, cut out the letters to make the word *orange*. Make each tall letter out of a 12″ x 18″ piece of paper and each small letter out of a 9″ x 12″ piece of paper. Put them on a wall with rubber cement at a level where the children can use them.

Provide scissors and magazines, and during center time have them cut out orange things from the magazines and glue them onto the letters.

As part of orange week, have a tasting party using as many orange foods as you can find. Many fruits and vegetables are orange, so another healthy party.

Demonstrate how to use a carrot peeler. Let the children peel the carrots and eat them. They can juice oranges or pour their own from a bottle.

During the week be sure to fly a flag denoting the color of the week. This week it could be an orange washcloth.

Have the children bring in labels that are orange which the children might read.

Go on an orange hunt to find all the orange things in the room and school.

25

GA1300

These pumpkins are orange.

1

2

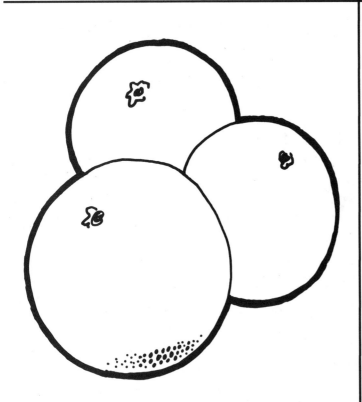

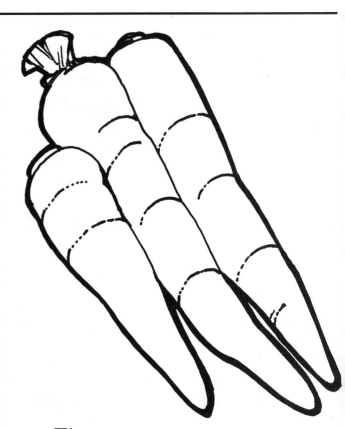

These oranges are orange.

These carrots are orange.

3

4

26

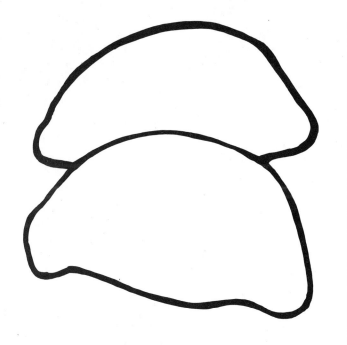

These sweet potatoes are orange.

5

These shoes are orange.

6

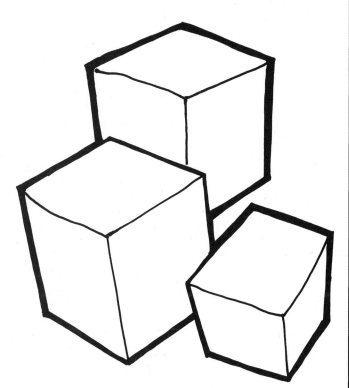

These blocks are orange.

7

Directions:
1. Listen to the story.
2. Color the pictures.
3. Cut out the pages.
4. Put the pages in order.
5. Staple the pages.
6. Read the story.

8

Orange

This is an orange _____

drawn by _____

28

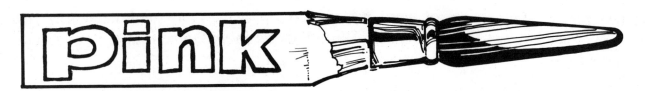

Dear Parents:

This week we will be watching for the color pink.

Your child has brought home a sack colored pink. Please look around your house for something that is pink to send to school. We will show the pink things to the other children.

Thanks for your help.

On the first day of the time scheduled to work on the color pink, have each child color a small white sack pink. Attach the note above after coloring the crayons pink. Send it home.

When the children return the sacks, have them show what they have in them.

Make the pink paper sack into a pink pig.

Stuff the sack with newsprint.

Tie a string around the top about 3″ down.

Cut the topknot into two parts.

Glue a pig's ear to each.

Give the children a piece of white poster board with the word *pink* written in such a way that they can fill in the letters. Have them fill in with glue rather than crayons. Sprinkle red tempera on the white glue and mix gently.

1. Trace 2. Glue 3. Sprinkle 4. Feel

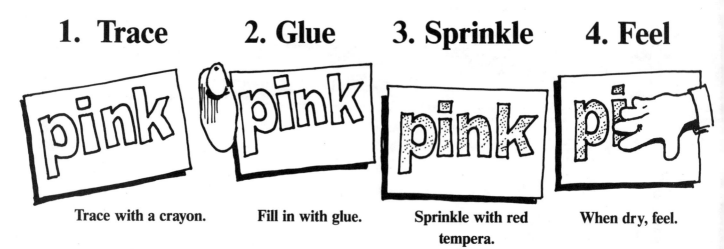

Trace with a crayon.   Fill in with glue.   Sprinkle with red tempera.   When dry, feel.

Before the children arrive at school, cut out the letters to make the word *pink*. Make each tall letter out of a 12″ x 18″ piece of paper and each small letter out of a 9″ x 12″ piece of paper. Put them up on a wall with rubber cement at a level where the children can use them.

Provide scissors and magazines, and during center time have children cut out pink things from the magazines and glue them onto the letters.

As part of pink week, have a tasting party using as many pink foods as you can find. Try pink icing on sugar cookies, pink grapefruit, pink lemonade, strawberry yogurt, strawberry ice cream, strawberry cream cheese, cotton candy. Serve these delicious pink foods buffet style on pink paper or plastic plates.

During the week be sure to fly a flag denoting the color of the week. This week it could be a pink scarf or washcloth.

Hunt for pink food labels which the children might read.

From one pink and two yellow circles, make a grapefruit in sections. The yellow circles should be slightly larger than the pink. Let the children cut the pink circle into sections and glue it onto the yellow circle. Tape the second yellow circle to the first at one edge. The grapefruit will then "open" to show the sections on the inside.

Pink

1

Color the pig pink.

2

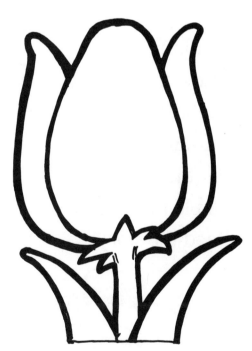

Color the flower pink.

3

Color the cotton candy pink.

4

31

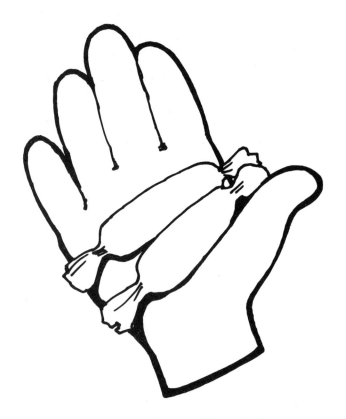

Color the taffy pink.

5

Color the lemonade pink.

6

Color the bunny's ears pink.

7

Directions:
1. Listen to the story.
2. Color the pictures.
3. Cut out the pages.
4. Put the pages in order.
5. Staple the pages.
6. Read the story.

8

GA1300

Pink

_____ mixed red and white to make pink.

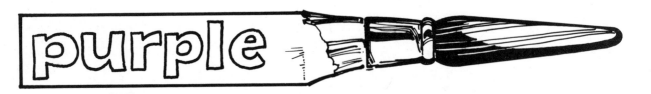

purple

Dear Parents:

Guess what the color of the week is this week? Right! You guessed it! Purple.

We are sending home a purple sack and ask that you send some purple things to school in it for sharing tomorrow.

The children certainly do enjoy hunting for purple things.

Thanks for your help.

On the first day of the time scheduled to work on the color purple, have each child color a small white sack purple. Send it home with the note above. Color the crayons purple before sending the note home.

When the children return the sacks, have them show what they have in them.

Make the paper sack into a Raisin Person.

Stuff the sack with newspaper.

Tie it shut as close to the top as possible.

Add eyes, nose and mouth.

Let the children design a hat for the head.

Legs can be made of toilet paper rolls.

Shoes can be stiff cardboard.

GA1300

Give the children a piece of white poster board with the word *purple* written in such a way that they will fill in the letters. Fill it in with glue mixed with grape Kool-Aid.

1. Trace   2. Glue   3. Smell

Trace with a crayon.   Fill in with smelly glue.   Smell.

Before the children arrive at school, cut out the letters to make the word *purple*. Make each tall letter out of a 12″ x 18″ piece of paper and each small letter out of a 9″ x 12″ piece of paper. Put them on a wall with rubber cement at a level where the children can use them.

Provide scissors and magazines, and during center time have them cut out purple things from the magazines and glue them onto the letters.

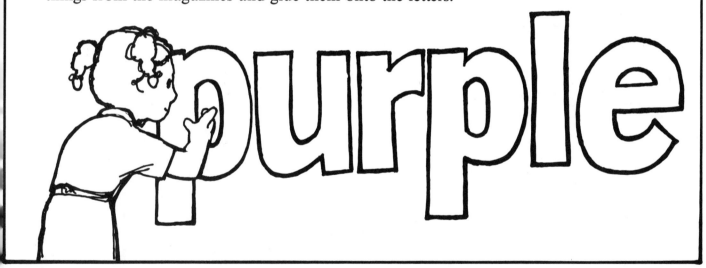

As part of purple week, have a tasting party using as many purple foods as you can find. Try plums, grapes, grape candy, grape Kool-Aid, grape Popsicles, grape jelly. Try making grape ice. Make the grape Kool-Aid and place it in ice trays or molds. Freeze. Put in a cup. Give children a fork to chop the ice into snow. Eat.

During the week be sure to fly a flag denoting the color of the week.

Look for purple food labels which the children might read. Have them go on a purple hunt in the school and on the playground. Record each thing they see on a piece of 4″ x 6″ white paper with purple marker. Write "A _____ is purple" at the bottom of the page. When they return to the room, illustrate each of the things they say. Staple them together. Make them into a book to place in the reading corner.

1

Color the grapes purple.

2

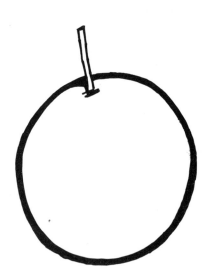

Color the plum purple.

3

Color the pants purple.

4

Color the sunset purple.

5

Color the hat purple.

6

Color the shoes purple.

7

Directions:
1. Listen to the story.
2. Color the pictures.
3. Cut out the pages.
4. Put the pages in order.
5. Staple the pages.
6. Read the story.

8

#

These grapes are purple.

38

red

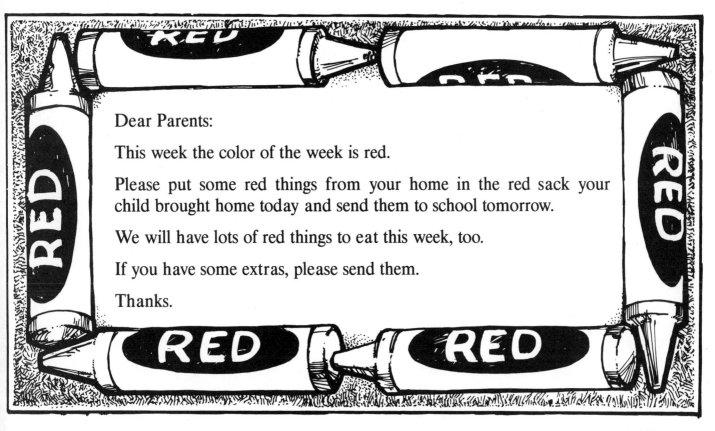

Dear Parents:

This week the color of the week is red.

Please put some red things from your home in the red sack your child brought home today and send them to school tomorrow.

We will have lots of red things to eat this week, too.

If you have some extras, please send them.

Thanks.

On the first day of the time scheduled to work on the color red, have each child color a small white sack red unless you can find inexpensive red sacks. Send it home with the note above. Color the crayons red before sending the note home.

When the children return the sacks, have them show what they have in them.

Make the paper sack into an apple.

Stuff the sack with newspaper.

Tie it shut 3″ from the top.

Add two green leaves to the top.

Hang from a large tree branch in the room.

Give the children a piece of white poster board with the word *red* written in such a way that they can fill in the letters. Fill it in with glue. Sprinkle with red sugar sprinkles. When dry, feel.

1. Trace

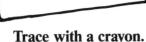

Trace with a crayon.

2. Glue

Fill in with glue.

3. Sprinkle

Sprinkle with red
sugar sprinkles.

4. Feel

Feel.

Before the children arrive at school, cut out the letters to make the word *red*. Make each tall letter out of a 12″ x 18″ piece of paper and each small letter out of a 9″ x 12″ piece of paper. Put them on a wall with rubber cement at a level where the children can use them.

Provide scissors and magazines, and during center time have them cut out red things from the magazines and glue them onto the letters.

Have a tasting party using as many red foods as you can find. Try strawberries, apples, cinnamon hearts, red bell peppers, tomatoes, pizza sauce, spaghetti sauce, Hawaiian Punch, pimentos, cherries, raspberries and red potatoes.

Make individual pizzas for snack. Spread sauce on an English muffin. Place cheese on top. Melt cheese in oven. Eat with cranberry juice.

During the week be sure to fly a flag denoting the color of the week. Try a red bandana.

Look for red food labels which the children might read.

Make a red mosaic apple.

Look for cardinals and red flowers on a red walk.

1

fire hat

2

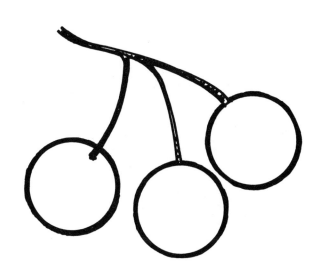

cherries

3

rose

4

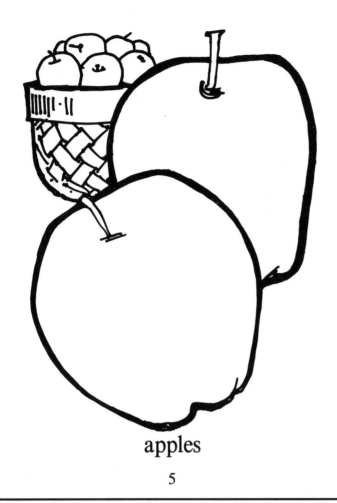

apples

5

Santa's hat

6

hearts

7

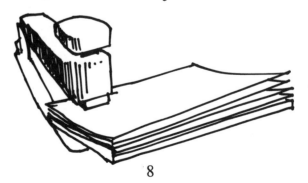

Directions:
1. Listen to the story.
2. Color the pictures.
3. Cut out the pages.
4. Put the pages in order.
5. Staple the pages.
6. Read the story.

8

42

GA1300

Red

What is red?
A valentine is red.

What is red?
A cardinal is red.

What is red?
An apple is red.

What is red?
A tomato is red.

What is red?
A rose is red.

What is red?
A hat is red.

43

GA1300

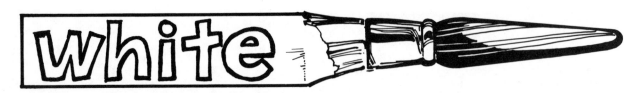

white

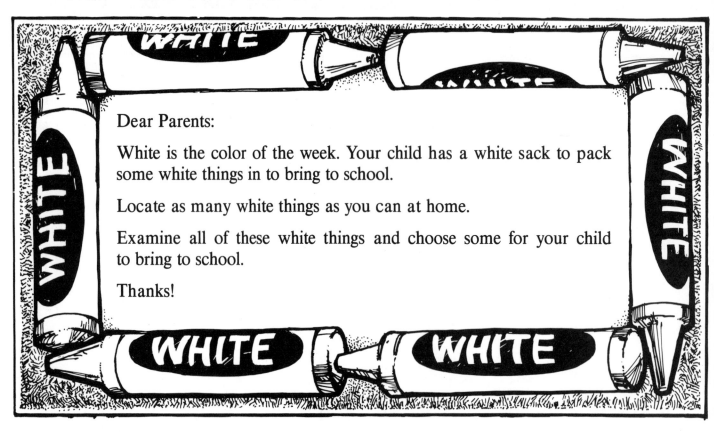

Dear Parents:

White is the color of the week. Your child has a white sack to pack some white things in to bring to school.

Locate as many white things as you can at home.

Examine all of these white things and choose some for your child to bring to school.

Thanks!

On the first day of the time scheduled to work on the color white, send home a white paper sack with each child. Attach the note above. Color the crayons white before sending the note home.

When the children return the sacks, have them show what they have in them.

Make the paper sack into a bunny.

Stuff the sack with newspaper.

Tie it shut 3″ from the top.

Cut the top into two parts. Tie the tops together.

Paint the ears pink.

Add eyes, nose and mouth. Use broom straws for whiskers.

44

GA1300

Give the children a piece of white poster board with the word *white* written in such a way that they can fill in the letters with glue. Sprinkle with rice.

1. Trace	2. Glue	3. Sprinkle
Trace with a crayon.	Fill in with glue.	Sprinkle with rice.

Before the children arrive at school, cut out the letters to make the word *white.* Make each tall letter out of a 12″ x 18″ piece of paper and each small letter out of a 9″ x 12″ piece of paper. Put them on a wall with rubber cement at a level where the children can use them.

Provide scissors and magazines, and during center time have them cut out white things from the magazines and glue them onto the letters.

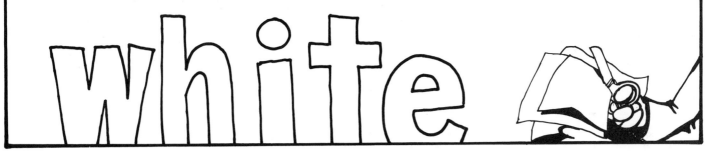

- Have a tasting party using as many white foods as you can find. Try sugar, flour, salt, bananas, potatoes, apples, onions, white cheese, egg white, ice cubes, popcorn, bread, marshmallows.

- For a snack try ice cream. You can make it in the classroom. Place a mixed recipe for ice cream in a baby food jar. Pack it tightly in a coffee can of ice and salt. Put a lid on and tape shut. Roll until frozen.

- During the week be sure to fly a flag denoting the color of the week. Try a white pillowcase.

- Look for white food labels which the children might read.

- Make an igloo out of ice cubes, shaking salt between the cubes and holding them until they refreeze. Freeze periodically in order that the whole thing does not melt.

1

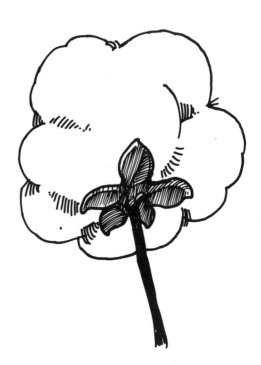

Look at the white cotton.

2

Look at the white cloud.

3

Look at the white potatoes.

4

Look at the white ghost.

5

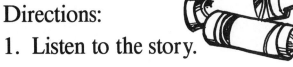

Look at the bride's white dress.

6

Look at the white bunny.

7

Directions:
1. Listen to the story.
2. Color the pictures.
3. Cut out the pages.
4. Put the pages in order.
5. Staple the pages.
6. Read the story.

8

47

GA1300

White

Look at my shiny white teeth.

White

Look at this fluffy white cloud.

GA1300

Yellow

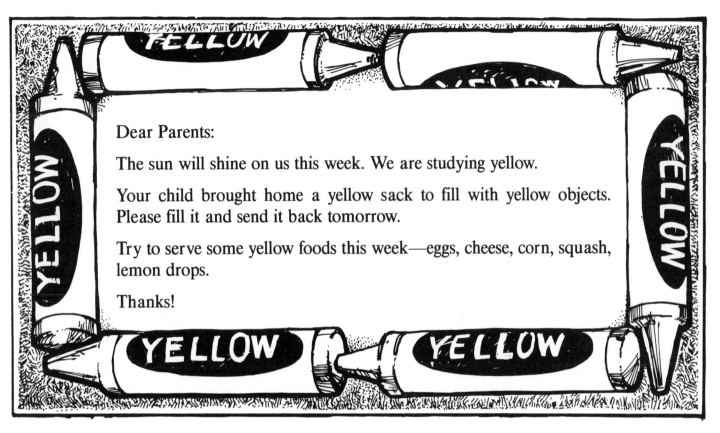

Dear Parents:

The sun will shine on us this week. We are studying yellow.

Your child brought home a yellow sack to fill with yellow objects. Please fill it and send it back tomorrow.

Try to serve some yellow foods this week—eggs, cheese, corn, squash, lemon drops.

Thanks!

On the first day of the time scheduled to work on the color yellow, send home with each child a white paper sack colored or painted yellow. Attach the note above. Color the crayons yellow before sending the note home.

When the children return the sacks, have them show what they have in them.

Make the paper sack into a lemon.

Stuff the bag with newspaper.

Tie it shut close to the top.

Squeeze and shape into a lemon shape.

Tie to a lemon tree—a tree branch of any tree will do.

GA1300

Give the children a piece of white poster board with the word *yellow* written in such a way that they can fill in the letters with glue. Sprinkle with dry mustard. Let it dry. Smell.

1. Trace and Glue   2. Sprinkle   3. Smell

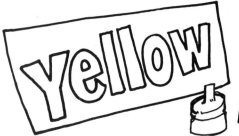  

Trace with a crayon.
Fill in with glue.

Sprinkle with dry mustard.

Smell.

Before the children arrive at school, cut out the letters to make the word *yellow*. Make each tall letter out of a 12″ x 18″ piece of paper and each small letter out of a 9″ x 12″ piece of paper. Put them on a wall with rubber cement at a level where the children can use them.

Provide scissors and magazines, and during center time have them cut out yellow things from the magazines and glue them onto the letters.

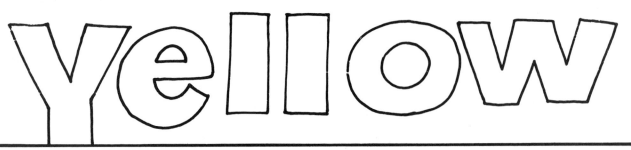

 Have a tasting party using as many yellow foods as you can find: lemons, squash, corn, lemon drops, banana, banana chips, cheese, butter, margarine, egg yoke, scrambled eggs.

Sunny Sun Snack
Cover sugar cookies with yellow icing. Place black licorice strips around the edges to make the rays of the sun.

During the week be sure to fly a flag denoting the color of the week. Try a yellow washcloth or yellow bandana.

Look for yellow food labels which the children might read.

Make a mosaic lemon out of yellow tissue paper.

Look for yellow birds in the pet shop and yellow flowers outside.

GA1300

Yellow

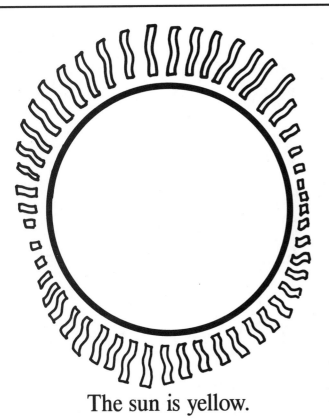

1

A banana is yellow.

2

The sun is yellow.

3

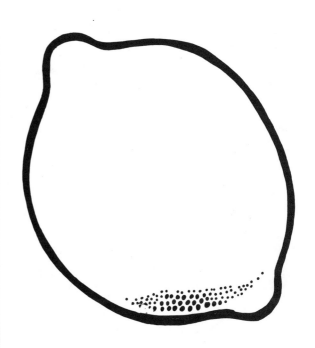

A lemon is yellow.

4

GA1300

A flower is yellow.

5

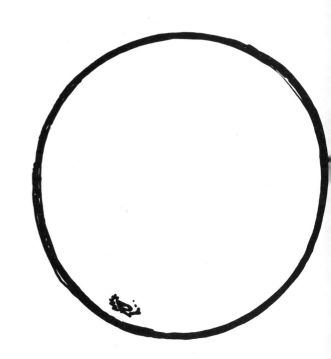

A grapefruit is yellow.

6

A lemon drop is yellow.

7

Directions:
1. Listen to the story.
2. Color the pictures.
3. Cut out the pages.
4. Put the pages in order.
5. Staple the pages.
6. Read the story.

8

Look at the yellow _____

drawn by _____ .

Rainbows

Rainbows can be found in a place other than the sky. In most instances water is a good source of color. The colors of the rainbow are in the order of red, orange, yellow, green, blue, indigo, and violet. Some say that you can remember this order by using the initials of each of the colors, Roy. G. Biv.

Another easy way to remember the colors of the rainbow is to remember the three primary colors in the pattern of red, yellow and blue repeated over and over: red, yellow and blue; red, yellow and blue; red, yellow and blue.

Note that between red and yellow comes orange, between yellow and blue comes green, and between blue and red comes purple. The only one left out is indigo, which is a dark portion between purple and blue. Have the children make a rainbow, using only the primary colors.

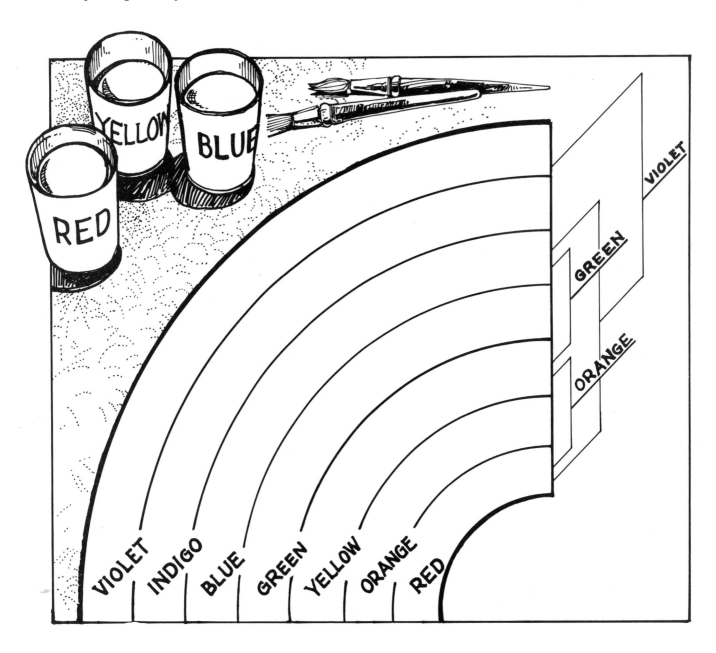

GA1300

Primary Color Rainbows

Demonstrate this process to the children as they watch in a small group or in the large group time. When you have completed the process, have them repeat to you the steps that you used, using this language pattern:

Paint a small red bow. Clean the brush.
Paint a yellow bow right next to the red bow. Clean the brush.
Paint a blue bow right next to the yellow bow. Clean the brush.
Paint a red bow right next to the blue bow. Clean the brush.

Materials:
watercolors, brushes and water
white painting paper,
—Use red to make the first (the smallest) bow of the rainbow, making sure that there is lots of red and lots of water in the brush.
—Clean the brush well.
—Use lots of yellow and lots of water in the brush and make the second bow slightly overlapping the first red bow.
—Clean the brush well.
—Use lots of blue and lots of water in the brush and make the third bow slightly overlapping the second yellow bow.
—To make the indigo and violet, add one final bow of red.
—As the paint dries, the colors will fade into one another making all the colors listed in the rainbow.

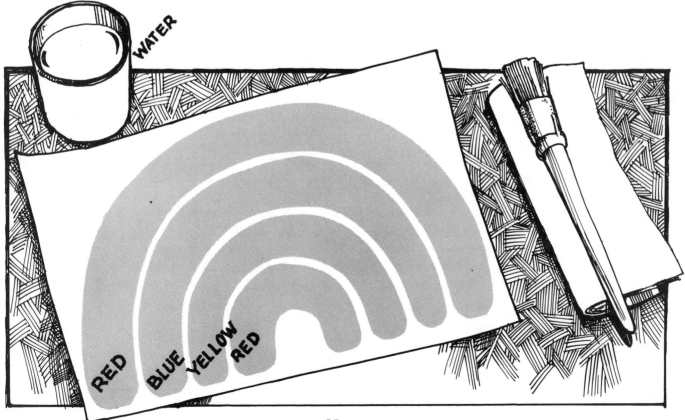

GA1300

Make a Rainbow

There are several ways that the children can experience the colors of the rainbow by making rainbows of their own. Most require water, sun, glass and a little vegetable oil.

Rainbow in My Room

Place a glass container of water in the window on a piece of white paper. As the sun shines through the water, a rainbow will form on the white paper. Be patient. The sun has to be at the right angle.

Rainbow Walk

Take the children on a rainbow walk. Give each child or each group of children a prism. As they walk about, have them hold the prism up to their eyes as they look at what is going on around them. The objects they examine will be outlined in a rainbow of color.

Oily Rainbows

After a rain, have the children observe how the oily spots on the ground, when covered with water, make a rainbow.

In order to make their own oily rainbows, have the children put a few drops of baby oil in a baby food jar filled with water. Hold this up to the light.

GA1300

Rainbow in a Spray Bottle

Remember the old story of the genie in the bottle? Well, a rainbow will come right out of a spray bottle of water if used just right. Give the children a spray bottle full of only water. Have them stand in the sunlight with the sun to their backs. Spray the water and watch for the rainbow. This also works with a hose, nozzle and water in a larger way.

Rainbow Crayons

Make rainbow crayons for the children to use. Take the paper off the rainbow colored crayons. Chop them into small pieces. Place a few of each color into miniature muffin tin cups. Melt in oven at 400 degrees 3-4 mintues. Cool. Color.

Soapy Rainbows

Give the children some water, dish soap and an eggbeater. Let them make a lot of bubbles with the eggbeater. Examine the bubbles for rainbows with a magnifying glass.

GA1300

Tissue Rainbows

Cut 1″ pieces of artist tissue in the seven colors of the rainbow. Have the children draw a rainbow and fill in with glue. Add the artist tissue in the right order. Overlap the colors if you want.

Bubble Bows

Good old liquid bubbles given for birthday presents are a good source of rainbows. Let the children blow bubbles outdoors on a lightly windy day. Let them chase the bubbles to see if one stops and lands on the ground. Examine it closely.

Color Me a Rainbow

Materials:
    crayons, griddle, good white paper

Have the children color a rainbow making the small red bow first, the yellow second and the blue third by coloring on the paper on a warm griddle and letting the colors blend into one another.

After they try it with just the three colors, have them try the red, orange, yellow, green, blue, indigo and violet. (Use a dark blue and black mix to make the indigo.)

Be sure to have an adult monitor the activity.

Make a Rainbow

Give the children these materials and see if they can find a way to make rainbows of their own: drinking glass, water, mirror.

Junk Rainbows

Have the children collect items for weeks that are the colors of the rainbow. Try cereals, dyed macaroni, things from nature, etc.

When it looks as if there is enough, have them make a junk rainbow as a class project.

Draw the lines to form a rainbow on a piece of large white butcher paper and let the children glue the right colors of objects onto the right bows (stripes).

GA1300

Rainbow Books

There are many books about rainbows that are suitable for young children. Be sure to use them throughout your study about colors and rainbows in particular.

Some good books with information and observations about rainbows:

Brown, C. *Noah's Ark*. Yellow Springs, OH: Antioch Publishing Co.

Brown, M. *Color Kittens*. New York, NY: Golden Press.

Lorimer, L. *Noah's Ark*. New York, NY: Random House.

Roloff, N. *The World Is a Rainbow of Color*. Colorado Springs, CO: Current, Incorporated.

Spier, P. *Noah's Ark*. Garden City, NY: Doubleday and Company.

_____. *Rain*. Garden City, NY: Doubleday and Company.

Some other good books to read:

Berenstain, J. & S. *The Berenstain Bears Get in a Fight*. New York, NY: Random House.

Freeman. *A Rainbow of My Own*. Viking Press.

Jablow, Alta, and Carl Withers. *Rainbow in the Morning*. New York, NY: Abelard-Schuman.

Johnson and Crockett. *Harold and the Purple Crayon*. New York, NY: Random House.

Walters. *Come and See the Rainbow*. Wonder Books.

Weston. *If I Only Had a Rainbow*. Weekly Reader Books.

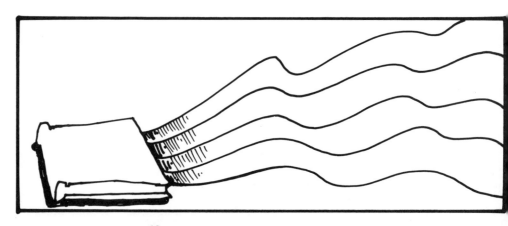

Some good books as teacher's resources:

Diebert, L. *Motivational Magic.* Carthage, IL: Good Apple, Inc., 1990.

Gleason, K. *Sunny Day Fun.* Carthage, IL: Good Apple, Inc., 1989.

GA1300

The Color of Me and Other Stuff

Have children examine themselves and then the others in the class for similarities and differences.

Hair Graphs

Have children look in mirrors in pairs and find partners who have hair the same or near the same color as theirs. When each has found a partner, have them sit in a spot away from the others.

Let them group themselves in larger groups.

Label the colors of hair that are in the room.

Have all with one color sit in one row.

Have all with another color sit in a second row, matching one to one with the first row.

When all rows are complete, stand on your desk and take a photo. This will make a graph picture of all the children's hair color.

When they can see the picture graph, have them make graphs themselves.

Use blank graph paper and color in the squares showing the number with each hair color.

Older children can first write the names of their friends in the right columns with black ink and then color in the color of the square.

Hair Graph

Write the names of the colors of hair of the children in your classroom in these bottom boxes.

Write the names of your classmates in the boxes above their appropriate colors. Color each box the right color.

Hair Colors in My Classroom
Questions to Be Answered Using the Hair Graph

1. Write the colors of hair found in your classroom.

   _____   _____

   _____   _____

   _____   _____

   _____   _____

2. Which color had the most? _____

3. Which color had the least? _____

   Who were they? _____

   _____   _____

   _____   _____

4. Were there any ties? _____

   If there were, what colors were tied?

   _____ tied with _____

   _____ tied with _____

5. Do you know of any other colors of hair that are not on your graph?

   Write them here.

   _____   _____

   _____   _____

GA130

Eye Graphs

Have the children look into mirrors and label their own eye colors. When they have identified the colors of their eyes, report to the teacher.

Line up the children in lines according to eye color. (It would be better to have them stand on a square drawn on a sheet or tarp as a graph.) Count the number of each eye color. Find the one with the most. The fewest.

Record the colors on an eye graph.

Older children can try to mix paints the exact color of their eyes and paint their eyes on a piece of paper. They can compare their eye colors to the others and be a bit more discriminating about the colors.

Skin Colors

Mix paints of white, peach, orange, tan.

Give each child a small Dixie cup, a paintbrush, a piece of white paper.

The job is to mix a color that is similar to the color of your own hand. Have children place their nonwriting hand down on the paper and trace around the arm and hand.

Have children mix the white, peach, orange and tan together and try to match it with their skin color. Color the traced hand and arm with their right skin color. Post all of these hands in a circle to form a circle of friends.

Eye Graph

Write the names of the colors of eyes of the children in your classroom in these bottom boxes.

Write the names of your classmates in the boxes above their appropriate colors. Color each box the right color.

GA1300

Eye Colors in My Classroom
Questions to Be Answered Using the Eye Graph

1. Write the colors of eyes found in your classroom in the eye color column and put the number of people with those colors in the number column.

_____ _____

_____ _____

_____ _____

_____ _____

_____ _____

_____ _____

_____ _____

Circle the color that had the most.

Underline the color that had the least.

2. Put the names of the colors of eyes in order starting with the one that had the most.

_____ _____

_____ _____

_____ _____

_____ _____

_____ _____

GA1300

What Color Are the Birds?

Have the children find and group pictures of birds that are of the same color. This study leads well into camouflage. Camouflage activities are found elsewhere in the book.

Blue	bluebirds and blue jays
Red	cardinals, redheaded woodpeckers, parrots, some pheasants
Green	parrots, parakeets, lovebirds, lapwings, hummingbirds
Yellow	parakeets, canaries, part of the toucan
Black	crows, Canadian geese, magpies, starlings, mynahs, toucans, wood-peckers, penguins, puffins, some swans
Dark Brown/ Black	geese, swallows, larks, pigeons, thrushes, quail, vultures, eagles, falcons, owls
White	ducks, swans, roosters, chickens, cockatoos, gulls, pelicans, cranes, storks

Make a bulletin board for the grouped pictures. Post all the birds of one color together and make a background for them that is their natural habitat, camouflaging them.

Bird Graph

Name _____

Go on a walk outside. Take a pencil with you. Look for birds.
When you see one, write the color of the bird in the small box at the bottom of the graph.
Put a tally mark in the box above the color word.
When you get back to the room, color the box.

GA1300

What Color Are the Flowers?

Have the children find and group pictures of flowers that are of the same color.

If you are in a place where there is a large variety of flowers in bloom at any one time, have the children bring flowers into the room and put them in vases by color. Put them in order of the colors of the rainbow: red, orange, yellow, green, blue, indigo, violet.

Label each flower in each vase.

Have children find more flowers in books and draw pictures of them to place near the real ones in the vases.

Yellow	sunflower, jonquil, tulip, daffodil, marigold, chrysanthemum, allamanda, jasmine, freesia, lilies
Red	rose, camellia, amaryllis, tulips, carnations, dahlia, poinsettia
Purple	rhododendron, iris, violets, primula, clematis, cup and saucer plant, crocus, alpine aster, water lily
Pink	roses, hydrangea, azalea, dahlia, snapdragons, periwinkle
Blue	cornflower, skyvine
Orange	dahlia, snapdragons, zinnias, marigold, rose, lily, rhododendron, tiger lily, begonia, pomegranate

Make a graph of the various types and colors of flowers. The graph should have the color at the bottom and the name of the type of flower in the box written with pencil. After the name of the flower is written in the box with pencil, color in the box with the color.

GA1300

Flower Graph

Name _____

	white	red	yellow	orange	green	blue	purple	black	brown	grey	
8											
7											
6											
5											
4											
3											
2											
1											

Go on a walk outside with your crayons. Look for flowers. When you see a flower, find the color word on the graph and write the name of the flower in one box above the color word. Then color the box. Go looking for other flowers and do the same.

71

GA1300

Camouflage

Which one is easier to see?
Hiding in colors is a fun activity for children to try. Animals do it all the time.

Place several sheets of colored butcher paper up along the wall.

Have a child who is dressed predominantly in red stand in front of the red paper. Have a child who is dressed predominantly in green stand in front of the blue paper.

Ask which one is easier to see?

After you do this with two or three children, have the children take charge of setting up the children in front of the paper.

Can you see?
Each of the following activities shows how difficult it is to see animals when they are in their natural habitat or when they are out of it.

White
On one sheet of white drawing paper, draw a picture of two polar bears or snowy owls. Cut out the pictures.
Glue one onto a sheet of white paper.
Glue the other on a sheet of black paper.
Glue both onto a 12″ × 18″ sheet of paper.
Write across the top "Can you see the polar bears?" or "Can you see the owls?"

Green

On one sheet of green construction paper, draw a picture of two grasshoppers or lizards. Cut out the pictures.

Glue one onto a sheet of green paper. Glue the other onto a sheet of black paper.

Glue both onto a 12″ × 18″ sheet of paper. Write across the top "Can you see the lizards?" or "Can you see the grasshoppers?"

Brown

On one sheet of tan drawing paper, draw a picture of two bears. Cut out the pictures.

Glue one onto a sheet of brown paper.

Glue the other onto a sheet of green paper.

Glue both onto a 12″ × 18″ sheet of paper. Write across the top "Can you see the grizzly bears?"

Ocean Critters

Give each child a piece of 12″ × 18″ blue paper. Give them scraps of blue, green, tan and yellow paper.

Have them make underwater plants, shells, fish, etc. Glue them onto the blue paper. Hide the animals from their predators.

GA1300

Tropical Forest

Give each child a sheet of 12″ × 18″ green paper. Give them scraps of brown, pink, coral, red and green paper.

Have them make trees, flowers, and plants out of the scraps and glue them onto the green paper to make a tropical forest.

Read about what animals and insects might live in a tropical forest. Cut these animals out of the right colors. Glue them onto the picture to make them fit right into the picture, hiding them as much as possible.

In the Pond

Give each child a piece of 12″ × 12″ brown paper. Have them cut off the edges to make a pond shape. Glue the pond shape onto a green sheet of 12″ × 18″ paper.

Have children tell you what animals and insects live near and in a pond. Have them cut them out and place them in the right places. Make sure the colors are correct.

74

Birds in a Nest

In most cases the male bird is much more colorful than the female. The female is more the color of the nest. Have children make a bird nest of construction paper. Make one for the state bird or a bird of your region. Let children draw a male and a female bird on white drawing paper. Place the female in the nest and the male away from the nest. Have the children explain why this placement is important for the bird family.

My Own Backyard

Have each child draw a picture of his own backyard or the backyard of the school ground.

Go on an insect hunt to find those creepy, crawly critters that live in the backyard. Take along crayons and draw them when you see them, trying to get them the right colors.

When you return to the room, cut out the creepy, crawly critters and place them on the drawn picture of My Own Backyard.

GA1300

Camouflage Coloring

Color this picture. Make sure that the animals are hidden from predators by coloring them the color of their natural background.

Colorful Experiments

Children will have a great time mixing colors in these experiments. Some are geared for younger children. Some are geared for older children. If you choose to do some geared for older children in a preschool classroom, do it as a demonstration with recorded results.

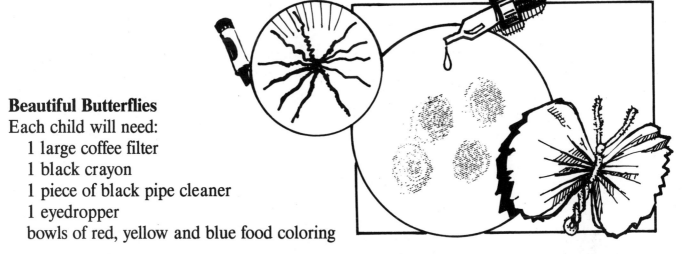

Beautiful Butterflies

Each child will need:
    1 large coffee filter
    1 black crayon
    1 piece of black pipe cleaner
    1 eyedropper
    bowls of red, yellow and blue food coloring

Draw lines with black crayon on the coffee filter to resemble the veins in the butterfly's wings.

Drop several drops of food coloring on the coffee filter, watching as they blend into one another.

When dry, twist a black pipe cleaner around the middle of the filter to bring the middle together making the filter into the two wings. The pipe cleaner becomes an antennae.

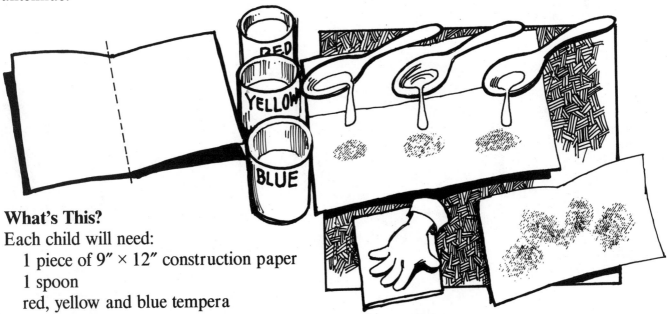

What's This?

Each child will need:
    1 piece of 9″ × 12″ construction paper
    1 spoon
    red, yellow and blue tempera

Fold the piece of paper in half. Open. Drop some paint of each color onto one half of the paper. Close the paper. Rub the outside of the paper several times with the palm of your hand or the side of a pencil. Open. What's this?

Pastel Pretties

Each child will need:

    1 piece of 9″ × 12″ black paper
    1 spoon
    1 eyedropper
    white, red, yellow and blue tempera

Fold the piece of paper in half. Open. Drop one spoonful of white paint onto one half of the paper. Place one drop of red, one drop of yellow and one drop of blue paint from the eyedropper in the middle of the spoonful of white paint. Close the paper. Rub the outside of the paper several times with the palm of your hand or the side of a pencil. Open. Examine and name the pastels.

Macaroni Mosaics

Dye the macaroni with the children or let them dye it by themselves.

To do this you need a mixture of food coloring and rubbing alcohol. The macaroni can be made into a necklace, or a mosaic of an apple (September), pumpkin (October), turkey (November), Christmas tree (December), heart (February), shamrock (March), rainbow (April), or a flower (May).

GA1300

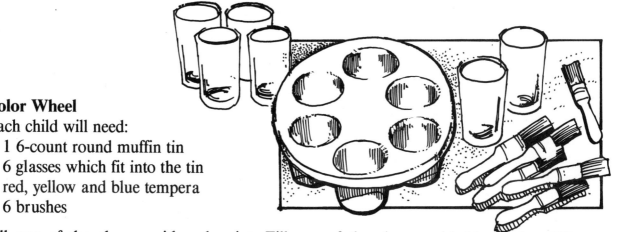

Color Wheel

Each child will need:
   1 6-count round muffin tin
   6 glasses which fit into the tin
   red, yellow and blue tempera
   6 brushes

Fill one of the glasses with red paint. Fill one of the glasses with blue paint. Fill one of the glasses with yellow paint. Put these three glasses in every other hole in the muffin tin.

Place the empty glasses in the other holes.

Pick up two of the glasses that have an empty glass in the middle. Pour a little of each into the empty glass. Replace the two glasses into their holes. Stir the new mixture with a brush.

Pick up two of the other glasses that have an empty glass in the middle. Pour a little of each into the empty glass. Replace the two glasses into their holes. Stir the new mixture with a brush.

Repeat to fill the third empty glass.

Divide a pizza wheel into six parts.

Paint the parts with the paint that you have made and put them in the same order that the muffin tin is in.

When the pizza wheel is dry, poke a hole in the middle with a tack. Attach this to an eraser. Spin it. What do you see?

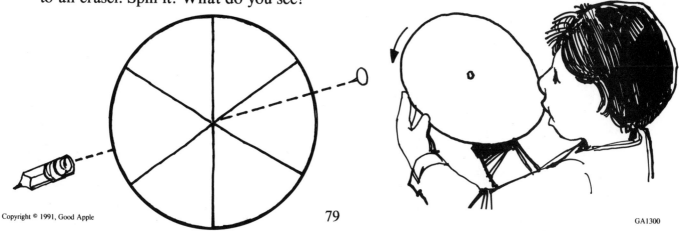

GA1300

Place Mats

Children can make their own place mats for the various seasons of the year. A new color experiment each month brings a new place mat.

Each child will need:

12″ × 18″ sheet of construction paper
cookie cutters or precut sponges of the season
2-3 colors of paint for the season
margarine lids on which to put the paint

Dip the cookie cutter or sponge into one color of paint and make several prints of it. Dip the cookie cutter or sponge into another color of paint and make several prints of it. Repeat to cover the entire sheet of paper. Let the paper dry. Cut it into the shape of the season—apple, pumpkin, turkey, etc., and laminate it to use at mealtime.

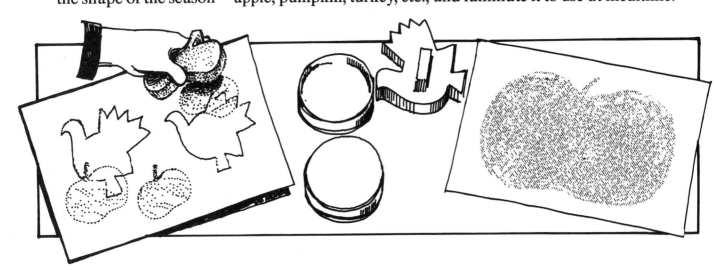

Fading Paper

Children can make colored water for any of the experiments by putting crepe paper into a baby food jar full of water. Test it frequently for the shade desired.

GA130

Soaking Celery (Climbing Colors)

As a whole-class experiment you will need:
  several stalks of celery
  glasses
  water
  red, yellow and blue food coloring

Cut off the bottom ends of the celery.
Place four stalks in a glass of red food coloring.
Leave for twenty-four hours.
Examine.
Record the results.

Leave one of the stalks in the red food coloring.

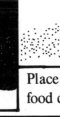

Take out three of the stalks.

Place two in yellow food coloring.

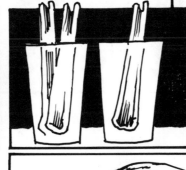

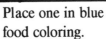

Place one in blue food coloring.

Leave for twenty-four hours.
Examine.
Record the results.

Leave one of the stalks in the yellow, but take one out and place it in the blue.

Leave for twenty-four hours.
Examine.
Record the results.
Isn't the celery mixed up?

GA1300

Colors Mixed Together Make New Colors

With only a box of crayons, children can mix colors and get amazing results. Try these activities at various times of the year.

Make fire under the witch's pot by coloring yellow first and then red on top of that and then blue.

Make the straw for Frosty's broom or the hay for the scarecrow by coloring yellow first and then brown streaks.

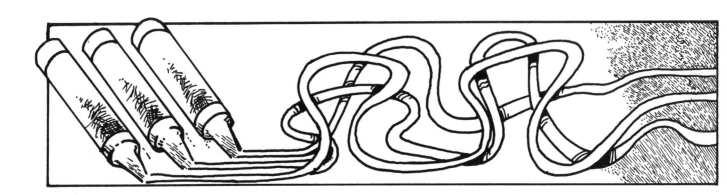

Make autumn trees by coloring the trunk brown and the leaves yellow. Make a second coat for the trunk with black. Make a second coat for the leaves with red. Make a third coat for the leaves with green.

GA130

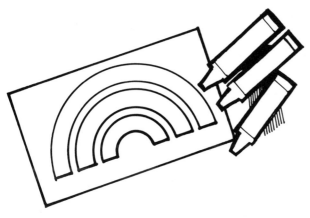

Crayon Rainbows

Each child will need:
    a rainbow stencil
    red, blue and yellow crayons
    1 sheet of 9″ × 12″ white paper

It will work best if children work in pairs for this project. One will hold the stencil on the paper and the other will color. They then switch places.

Place the stencil on the paper. Color in arcs first with yellow. Color in arcs next with red. Color in arcs last with blue. Look at all the colors that are made with only three crayons.

Mixed Up Marble Painting

Hearts for Valentine's Day

To make hearts for Valentine's Day, give each child a heart-shaped piece of paper. Place the paper in a cake pan or sided-cookie sheet. Dip marbles in white and red paint. Place three marbles of each color onto the heart. Tip the pan just right to make the marbles roll. Watch the mixing of colors.

Rainbows

To make rainbows to brighten up any day, give each child a rainbow-shaped piece of paper. Place the paper in a cake pan or sided-cookie sheet. Dip marbles in red, yellow and blue paint. Place three marbles of each color onto the rainbow. Tip the pan just right to make the marbles roll. Watch the mixing of colors.

GA1300

More Mixed Up Marble Painting

Trees

To make fall trees for the bulletin board, give each child a treetop-shaped piece of paper. Children can tear their own from a 9″ × 12″ piece of white paper. Place the paper in a cake pan or sided-cookie sheet. Dip marbles in red and yellow paint or yellow and blue paint. Place three marbles of each color onto the treetop. Tip the pan just right to make the marbles roll. Watch the mixing of colors. When dry, cut out a tree trunk from brown paper and glue to the treetop. Post in the hall.

Easter Eggs

To make Easter eggs to fit in a large bulletin board basket, give each child an egg-shaped piece of paper. Place the paper in a cake pan or sided-cookie sheet. Dip marbles in white, red, yellow and blue paint. Place three marbles of white and three marbles of one other color onto the egg-shaped piece of paper. Tip the pan just right to make the marbles roll. Watch the mixing of colors and the making of pastels.

84

GA1300

Mixed Up Glasses

Children can get a look at the world through mixed up glasses. To make the glasses, cut the bottoms off of six Styrofoam cups. On two put yellow cellophane. On two put red cellophane. On two put blue cellophane.
Let the children experiment.

Hold up the two yellow to the eyes and look at the world.
Hold up the two red to the eyes and look at the world.
Hold up the two blue to the eyes and look at the world.

Now stack them. Stack the yellow on the blue. Look around.

Stack the red on the yellow. Look around.

Mix up the glasses in whatever way you want and take a look around.

GA1300

Colorful Food

Pancakes
Add food coloring to pancakes.

More than one color can be added to each pancake. Children can swirl the colors together. Cook and eat them.

Colorful Jell-O
Make pans of Jell-O of various colors.

When firm, cut into cubes. Take a spoonful of each and put into individual Dixie cups.

Let the children observe, mix and eat the colorful Jell-O.

Cupcakes
Bake white cupcakes that have had food coloring swirls made in them right before placing in the muffin cups.

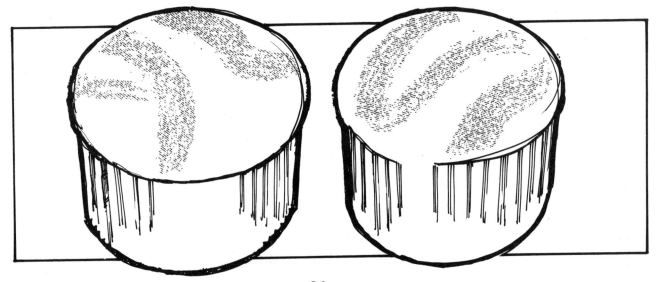

GA130C

Color Mixing

Experiment 1

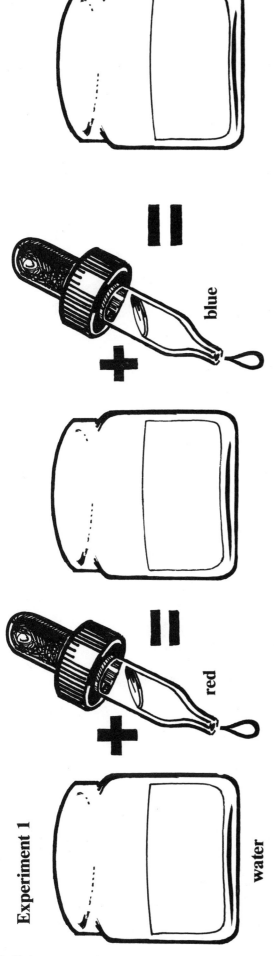

water + red =

red + blue =

Experiment 2

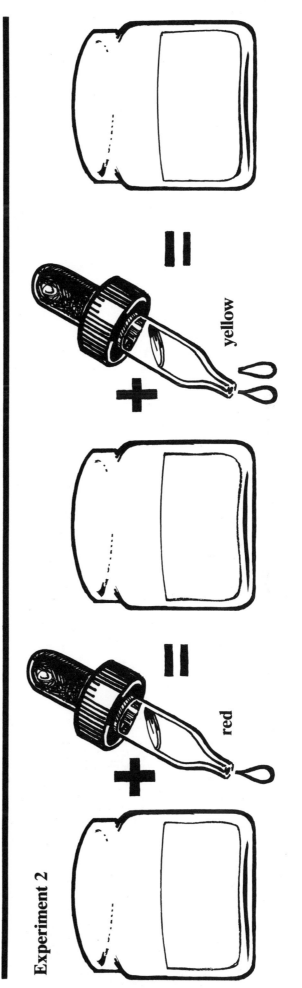

red =

yellow =

Follow the directions for these written experiments. Record your results by coloring in the water and eyedroppers correctly.

GA1300

Color Mixing

Name _____

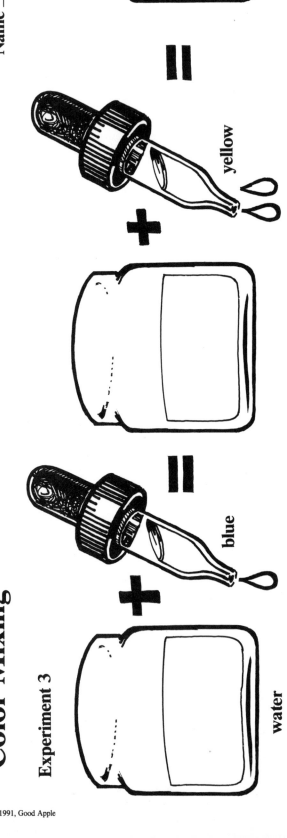

Experiment 3

water **+** blue **=**

+ yellow **=**

Follow the directions for this written experiment. Record your results by coloring in the water and eyedroppers correctly.

Make up your own experiment using the colors you choose and the number of drops that you choose.

Experiment 4

water **+** *Choose the color and number of drops. Write the color.* **=**

+ *Choose the color and number of drops. Write the color.* **=**

September Apple Cookie

Mix 1

tablespoon

White Icing

with

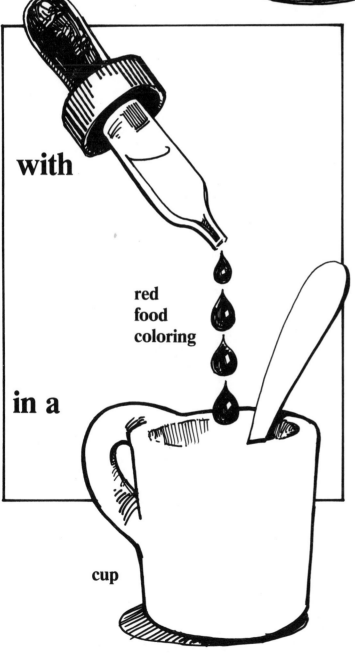

red
food
coloring

in a

cup

Spread on 1

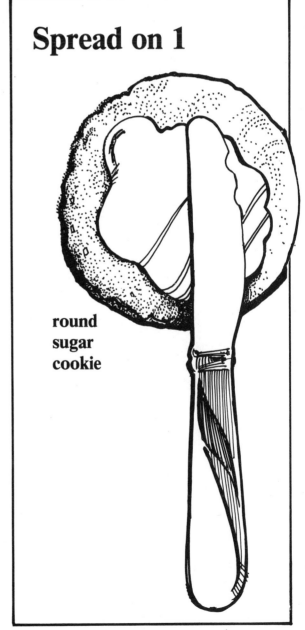

round
sugar
cookie

October Pumpkin Cookie

Mix 1

tablespoon

White Icing

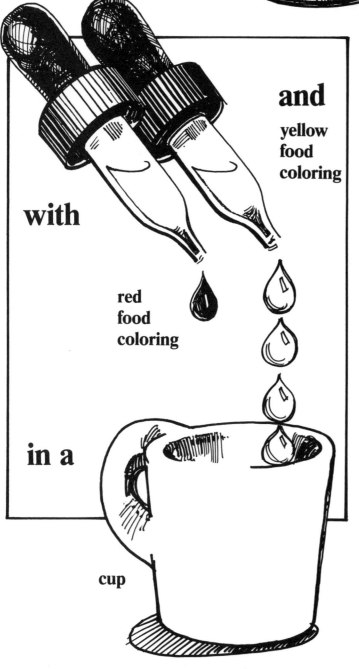

with

red
food
coloring

and

yellow
food
coloring

in a

cup

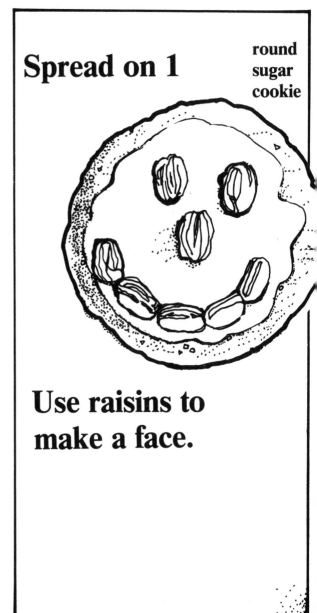

Spread on 1

round
sugar
cookie

**Use raisins to
make a face.**

November Leaf Cookie

Swirl 1

tablespoon

White Icing

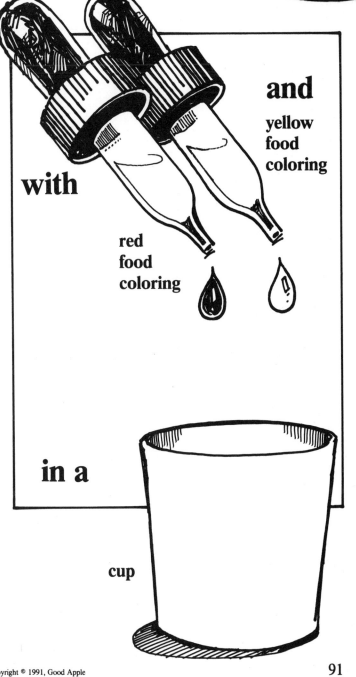

with

red
food
coloring

and

yellow
food
coloring

in a

cup

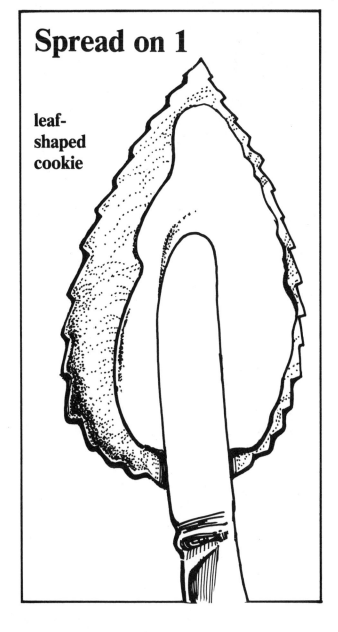

Spread on 1

leaf-
shaped
cookie

91

December Ornament Cookie

Mix 1

tablespoon

White Icing

with

green
food
coloring

in a

cup

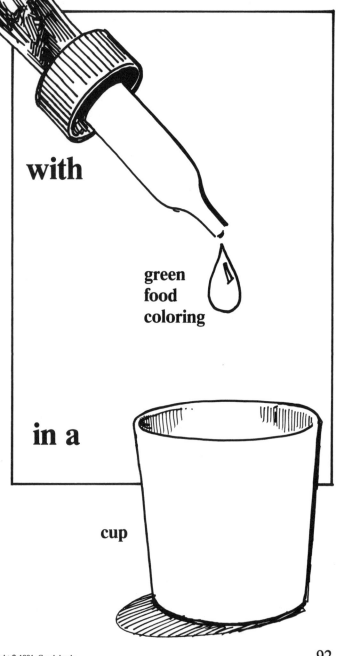

Spread on 1

round
sugar
cookie

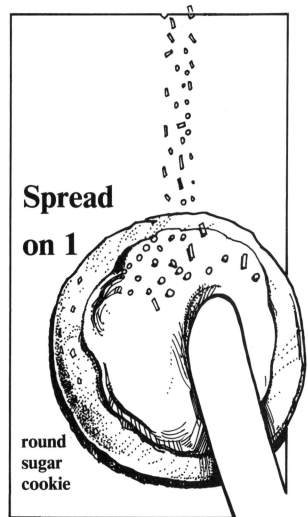

Sprinkle with silver sprinkles to make it shine.

92

January Snowman Cookie

Spread 1

tablespoon

White Icing

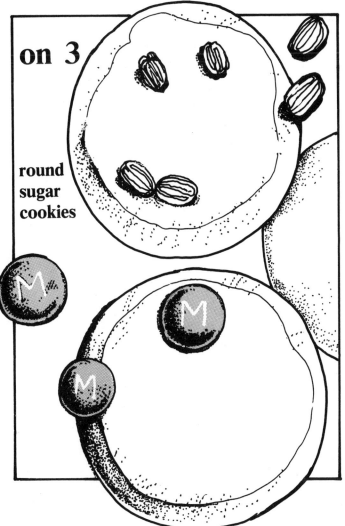

on 3

round sugar cookies

Put raisin eyes, nose and mouth on 1.

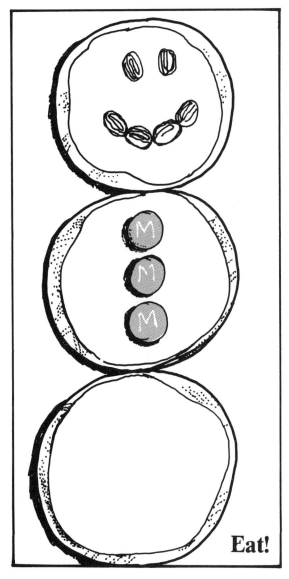

Place M & M buttons on 1. Shape all 3 like a snowman.

Eat!

February Heart Cookie

Mix 1

tablespoon

White Icing

with

red
food
coloring

in a

cup

Spread on 1

heart-
shaped
cookie

94

March Shamrock Cookie

Mix 1

tablespoon

White Icing

with

green
food
coloring

in a

cup

Spread on 1

shamrock-shaped
sugar
cookie

GA1300

April Egg Cookie

Spread 1

on 1
egg-shaped
sugar cookie

tablespoon

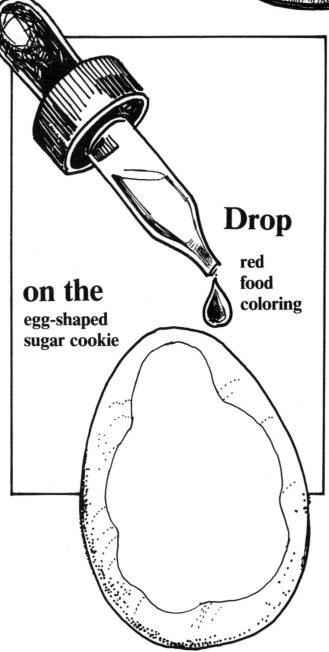

Drop
red
food
coloring

on the
egg-shaped
sugar cookie

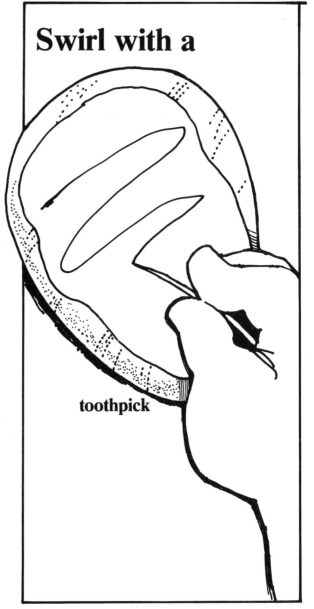

Swirl with a

toothpick

96

GA1300

May Flower Cookie

Mix 1

tablespoon

White Icing

with

yellow
food
coloring

in a

cup

Spread on 1

sugar
cookie

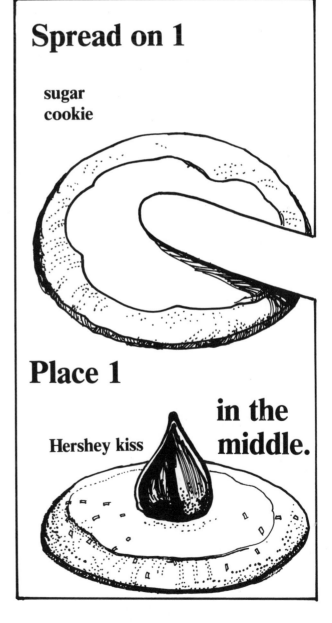

Place 1

Hershey kiss

**in the
middle.**

Creative Crayons

The activities on the following few pages are designed for use with older children, late first grade or second and third grades.

Crayons are something we all have in the classroom, and they are something that the children can use creatively. Each of the activities on the following pages allows for the children to use crayons in different ways.

As you prepare the children to use these activities, demonstrate the process with them using the bottom of the sheet to record what the project will look like.

If you do them one at a time, demonstrate and then let the children color. If you choose, demonstrate several at a time and have centers set up around the room and let the children move from area to area.

1. Make a pattern of any shape and/or size from a thick piece of paper.

2. Place it on a blank piece of paper.

3. Use crayons to draw an edge around the pattern.

4. With a dry tissue, rub the color onto the piece of paper.

5. Do this several times with the same or different colors.

Note to teacher: Demonstrate and make a sample at the bottom of the page.

GA1300

1. You can make a wonderful pattern of dots by dripping light-colored hot wax crayon on a dark sheet of drawing paper.

2. The candle must be held in one hand and the crayon in the other.

3. The crayons harden so quickly they must be held in the flame over the drawing paper until the hot wax drips directly onto the paper.

Note to teacher: Demonstrate and make a sample at the bottom of the page.

1. Think of a picture you would like to draw that is large and mostly one color.

2. Draw the picture with crayons, pressing firmly.

3. After the picture is completed, rub the crayon with wadded paper until some of the color smears out into the background, creating a special effect of color tones. This must be done carefully so that the smears add to the picture. It doesn't work if you just scrub around anywhere.

Note to teacher: Demonstrate and make a sample at the bottom of the page.

GA1300

1. Draw a picture of an object.

2. Use a second color. Make a "star burst" out from the object.

3. Use a third color. Make a "star burst" out from the previous one.

4. Continue until you reach the outer edge of the paper.

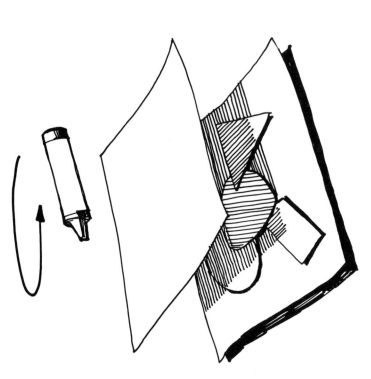

Note to teacher: Demonstrate and make a sample at the bottom of the page.

---

1. Cut out several shapes from oaktag.

2. Paste them on a piece of paper.

3. Place another sheet of paper over the pattern.

4. Rub a crayon over all layers.

5. Use as many different colors as you want on the same piece of paper.

Note to teacher: Demonstrate and make a sample at the bottom of the page.

1. Draw a picture pressing firmly.

2. Rub the crayon with wadded paper smearing it carefully to make special effects.

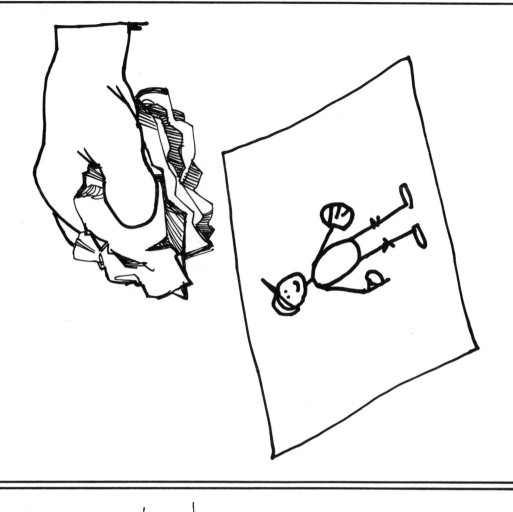

1. Draw a picture using colored chalk.

2. Color over that with white crayon.

3. Color over the white with black crayon.

4. Cover the drawing with another piece of paper.

5. Draw a picture on the second piece of paper by pressing the pencil firmly.

GA1300

1. Draw a picture, pressing your crayon firmly.

2. Color over the picture with a black crayon.

3. Using a comb, pull in one direction across the paper several times until most of the black is gone.

Note to teacher: Demonstrate and make a sample at the bottom of the page.

1. Draw a picture with colored chalk.

2. Cover this entire picture with white crayon.

3. Place a piece of colored paper over this first page.

4. Draw a picture on this page with pencil being sure to press it firmly.

Note to teacher: Demonstrate and make a sample at the bottom of the page.

GA1300

1. Draw a picture on a piece of sandpaper.

2. Place a piece of paper over the sandpaper.

3. Put this between two sheets of newspaper.

4. With a hot iron, press the picture firmly.

5. This will make two pictures which may be mounted together or separately.

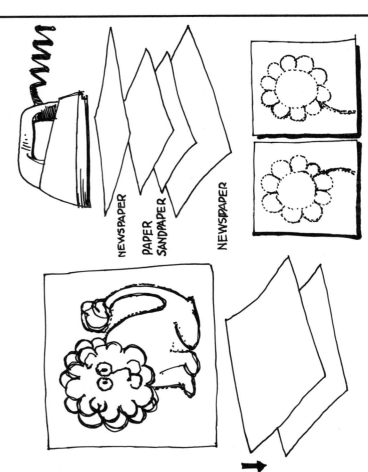

NEWSPAPER

PAPER
SANDPAPER

NEWSPAPER

Note to teacher: Demonstrate and make a sample at the bottom of the page.

---

1. Shave some crayons with a plastic seriated knife.

2. Place the shavings between two sheets of wax paper.

3. Place these between two sheets of newspaper.

4. Iron the paper to melt the crayons.

5. Make a pattern of the season on the wax paper.

6. Cut it out.

7. Hang it in a window.

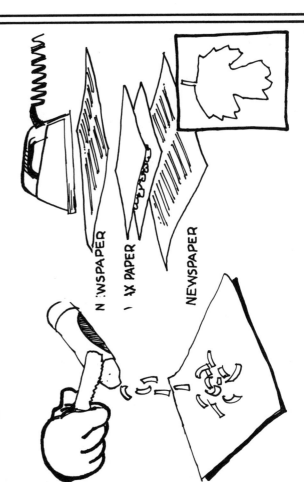

NEWSPAPER

WAX PAPER

NEWSPAPER

Note to teacher: Demonstrate and make a sample at the bottom of the page.

GA1300

1. Draw a funny animal.

2. Tear out the animal.

3. Glue it onto a sheet of white paper.

4. Tear the animal out of this paper leaving a border around your first animal.

5. Glue both on another sheet of construction paper.

Note to teacher: Demonstrate and make a sample at the bottom of the page.

1. Draw a picture of a funny looking animal. Use only three or four colors.

2. When the picture is complete, tear it out from the extra paper.

3. Choose a piece of construction paper that matches one of the colors in your picture.

4. Tear out a piece of construction paper which is larger than the torn piece with the animal on it.

5. Mount the animal on the construction paper.

Note to teacher: Demonstrate and make a sample at the bottom of the page.

Natural Dyes

Children will love to learn that they can color with things that are in their environment, that they see every day at home, and that are free of charge. Dyes from objects in nature can be great fun.

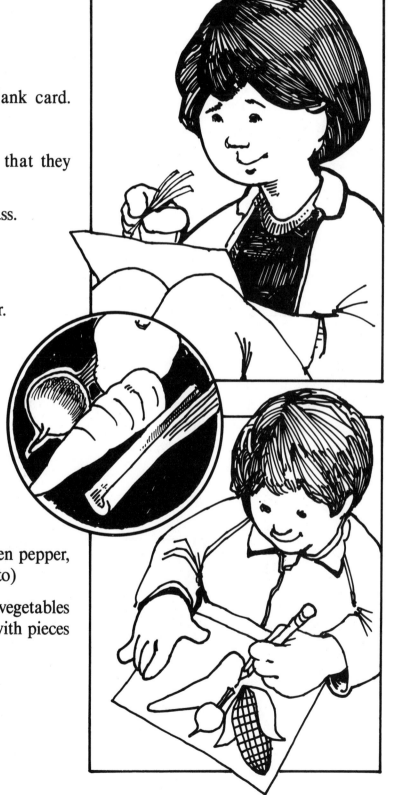

Natural Paintings

Give each child a 5″ × 8″ white blank card.

Go outside for a walk.

Let them draw pictures using things that they can see and pick up.

Use grass to smear on the sheet as grass.

Use dirt to make a tree trunk.

Use a leaf to smear on as leaves.

Use a leaf to make a stem for a flower.

Use a flower to smear on as a flower.

Vegetable Paintings
Materials:
    1 piece of thick paper
    vegetables cut into pieces
        (carrot, red cabbage, radish, green pepper,
        celery, corn, squash, sweet potato)

Have children draw pictures of these vegetables with their pencils and color them in with pieces of raw vegetables.

GA1300

Spring Bookmarks

Materials:

    1 cup rubbing alcohol
    dandelion blossoms (lots of them)
    old sheeting pinked into 1½″ × 8″ strips
    (new 100% cotton washed muslin can be used)

Let the children pick the dandelion blossoms from a few branches of the dandelion plant. After they are picked, squash, smash, squeeze them and place them in one cup of rubbing alcohol. Add the strips of sheeting. Soak overnight. Take out. Dry, iron, use as book-marks.

Variations:

1. Stick your finger up into, but not through, the strip of material in a few places. Wrap a rubber band around these spots before placing the material in the dye.

2. Dye the material in one color. Stick your finger up into, but not through, the strip of material in a few places. Wrap a rubber band around these spots before placing the material into a second color of dye.

GA1300

Colorful Bows

Materials:
    1 cup rubbing alcohol
    red cabbage or carrots (lots of them)
    old sheeting pinked into 4″ × 6″ rectangles
    (new 100% cotton washed muslin can be used)

Chop up red cabbage or carrots and squash, smash, squeeze the pieces.
Place the carrots in one cup of rubbing alcohol.
Place the red cabbage in another cup of rubbing alcohol.

Add the pieces of cloth. Soak overnight. Take out. Dry, iron and squeeze together in the middle.
Tie with a piece of colorful ribbon to make the middle of the bow.
Stitch or hot glue to a barrett.

Variations:
1. Stick your finger up into, but not through, the piece of material in a few places. Wrap a rubber band around these spots before placing the material in the dye.

2. Dye the material in one color. Stick your finger up into, but not through, the strip of material in a few places. Wrap a rubber band around these spots before placing the material into a second color of dye.

GA1300

Color each crayon the right color.   Write the color word on the line.

red   _____

yellow   _____

blue   _____

orange   _____

green   _____

purple   _____

pink   _____

brown   _____

black   _____

white   _____

tan   _____

gray   _____

                   GA1300

What Color Should It Be?

Trace around each of the pictures below with the color it should be. Be sure to press hard when you trace.

Color each picture in with the same color, but color lightly.

Write the color word on the line below the picture.

_____

_____   _____

_____   _____

Writing Color Words

On each of the crayons write a color word with your pencil.

Color the crayon the right color after you write the color word on the crayon.

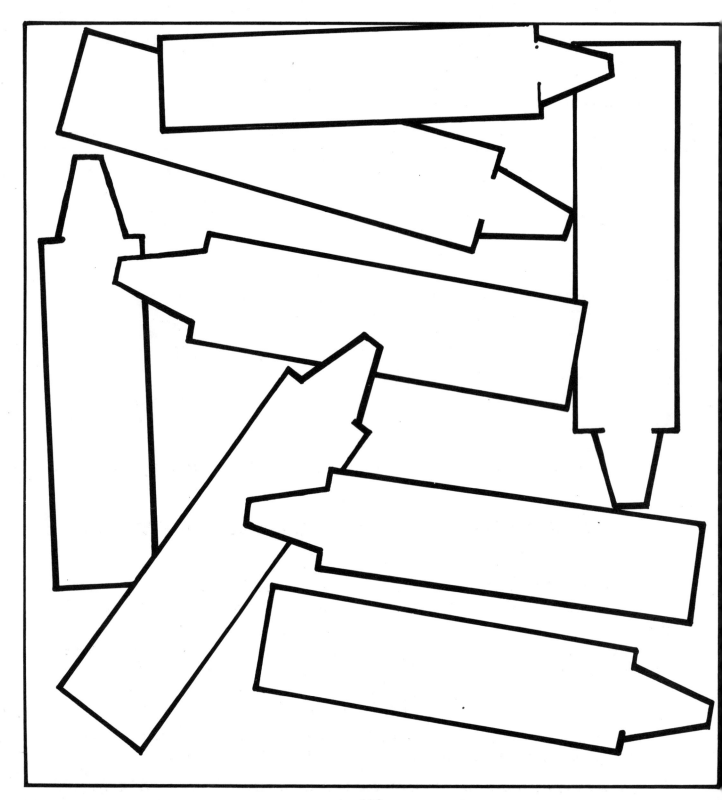